www.heinemann.co.uk/library
Visit our website to find out more information about **Heinemann Library** books.

To order:
☎ Phone 44 (0) 1865 888066
▤ Send a fax to 44 (0) 1865 314091
🖳 Visit the Heinemann Bookshop at www.heinemann.co.uk/library to browse our catalogue and order online.

J623.7464
1450123

First published in Great Britain by Heinemann Library, Halley Court, Jordan Hill, Oxford, OX2 8EJ, part of Harcourt Education.
Heinemann is a registered trademark of Harcourt Education Ltd.

Editorial: Andrew Farrow and Dan Nunn
Design: Jo Hinton-Malivoire and Tinstar Design Limited (www.tinstar.co.uk)
Illustrations: Geoff Ward
Picture Research: Rebecca Sodergren and Bob Battersby
Production: Viv Hichens

Originated by Dot Gradations Ltd
Printed and bound in China by South China Printing Company

ISBN 0 431 16561 0
07 06 05 04 03
10 9 8 7 6 5 4 3 2 1

British Library Cataloguing in Publication Data

Graham, Ian, 1953 –
  Attack Fighters. – (Designed for Success)
  1. Fighter planes – Juvenile literature
  2. Attack planes – Juvenile literature
  I. Title
  623.7'464
A full catalogue record for this book is available from the British Library.

Acknowledgements

The publishers would like to thank the following for permission to reproduce photographs: API p. **25** (top); Aviation Picture Library pp. **5** (top), **11**, **16**; Aviation Picture Library/Austin J. Brown p. **26**; Corbis pp. **15** (bottom), **20**, **21** (top); Corbis/Roger Ressmeyer p. **10** (top); Defense Visual Information Center pp. **12** (top), **13** (top); EPA pp. **1**, **9** (top), **15** (top), **18**; Flight Collection pp. **19** (top), **19** (bottom), **28**; Flight Collection/Erik Simonsen pp. **3**, **27** (bottom); Flight Collection/Mark Wagner p. **10**; MPL p. **25** (bottom); Pratt & Whitney pp. **17** (top), **17** (bottom); Skyscan Photo Library/Chris Allan pp. **22**, **24**; TRH Pictures pp. **6**, **9** (bottom), **13** (bottom), **23**, **27** (top); TRH Pictures/Douglas McDonnell pp. **4** (bottom), **4** (top); TRH Pictures/Lockheed Martin p. **14**; TRH Pictures/Macdonald p. **24** (middle); TRH Pictures/Paul Reynolds p. **5** (bottom); TRH Pictures/Peter Holman pp. **17** (middle); TRH Pictures/Peter Modigh p. **7** (top); TRH Pictures/US National Archives p. **29**.

Cover photograph, reproduced with permission of Corbis (plane) and Getty Images (background).

Every effort has been made to contact copyright holders of any material reproduced in this book. Any omissions will be rectified in subsequent printings if notice is given to the publishers.

Disclaimer

CONTENTS

Any words appearing in the text in bold, **like this**, are explained in the Glossary.

ATTACK FIGHTERS

Fighters are small, fast, well-armed jet aeroplanes. They are designed to attack other aircraft. New fighters are being developed all the time to make them better and better.

The American F-15 Eagle set new standards for modern fighters when it was designed in the 1960s. It flew for the first time in 1972. Its speed and **manoeuvrability** meant that it could out-fly any other fighter in the world. The F-15 is a type of aircraft called an **'air-superiority' fighter**. Its job is to clear the sky of enemy aeroplanes. Fighters often do other work, too – fighter-bombers and strike fighters can attack targets on the ground.

AIR-TO-AIR COMBAT

The F-15 attacks other aeroplanes with a cannon (a type of aircraft machine-gun) and up to eight missiles. The cannon can fire up to 100 rounds a minute. The missiles are carried under the wings and body. The missiles can be a mixture of:
- AIM-7 'Sparrows'
- AIM-9 'Sidewinders'
- AIM-120 AMRAAMs (Advanced Medium-Range Air-to-Air Missiles).

STRIKE EAGLE

The F-15 can work as an **interceptor**, an aeroplane that flies a long way at top speed to meet incoming fighters or bombers and stop them. It was so successful that a new type of F-15 was developed that could also attack targets on the ground. This version is called the F-15E Strike Eagle.

SINGLE-SEATER

The F-15 was originally intended to have a crew of two. However, the **cockpit** design was changed to enable one pilot to fly it. All the switches that controlled the weapons were fitted to the pilot's control **stick**. This enabled him to fire the aeroplane's weapons without taking his hands off the flight controls. The second crewman, the weapons officer, wasn't needed any more. So, the F-15 became a single-seater.

When the F-15E Strike Eagle fighter-bomber was developed, the aeroplane's weapons became even more complicated. The pilot could no longer do everything unaided. So, a second seat and cockpit were installed behind the pilot for a weapons officer.

IN-FLIGHT REFUELLING

An F-15E can be refuelled without landing. A tanker-aeroplane trails out a hose behind it. The end plugs into a socket on the left side of the F-15E. Fuel flows from the tanker into the F-15E's tanks. In-flight refuelling means that an F-15E can fly for as long or as far as it needs. It is not limited by the size of its fuel tanks.

F-15E Strike Eagle

Type: strike fighter-bomber
Country: USA
Crew: 2
Wingspan: 13.1 metres
Top speed: 2655 kmph (1650 mph)
Max weight: 36,740 kg
Max weapon load: 11,110 kg

DESIGNING FIGHTERS

The design of a fighter depends on the sort of job it has to do. Designers try to produce fighters that out-perform any enemy aircraft and other defences they might meet.

Fighters have to be able to chase enemy aeroplanes and also escape from aeroplanes that attack them. Being able to turn very tightly helps them to do this and win air battles called dogfights. A super-fast top speed isn't so important for dogfighting because slower aeroplanes can turn more tightly. However, some fighters that are designed to do other jobs are very fast indeed. **Interceptors** have a very high top speed so that they can reach approaching enemy aeroplanes as quickly as possible when they are still far away from their targets. Most can fly at twice the speed of sound. A few, including the Russian MiG-25 and MiG-31, can top three times the speed of sound – that's more than 3000 kph (1900 mph)!

JOINING FORCES

As its name suggests, the Eurofighter is a fighter built by a group of European aeroplane-makers. Britain, Spain, Germany and Italy shared the work and the huge cost of developing the new fighter. France was involved at the beginning, but left to develop its own fighter, called Rafale. Eurofighter is an **air-superiority fighter**, designed to do the same job as the F-15.

GRIPEN

The Saab Gripen is a Swedish multi-role fighter. It's designed to fly three different types of missions:
- It can fight other aircraft.
- It can attack targets on the ground.
- It can spy on the enemy (called reconnaissance).

The Gripen can be prepared for a new mission by only five people, and within just 10 minutes of landing!

This Gripen is on a mission over the snow-covered terrain of northern Sweden.

Control surfaces

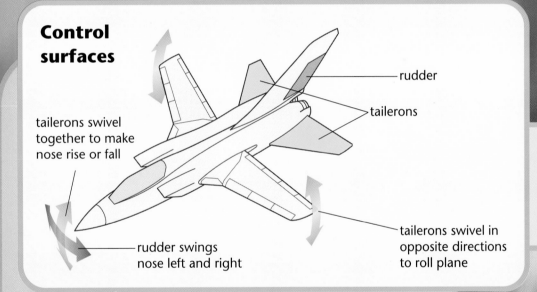

tailerons swivel together to make nose rise or fall

rudder

tailerons

rudder swings nose left and right

tailerons swivel in opposite directions to roll plane

This illustration shows an aircraft that is controlled using tailerons.

STEERING AEROPLANES

A pilot steers by moving parts of an aeroplane's wings and tail called **control surfaces**. When the **rudder** or the **tail-fin** swivels to one side, air rushing past the aeroplane hits it and swings the tail round. Swivelling the **elevators** or the **tail-planes** makes the aeroplane climb or dive. **Ailerons** in the wings swivel in opposite directions, making the aeroplane roll. Sometimes one part does two jobs. Tail-planes that do the ailerons' job too are called tailerons. Wing flaps that work as ailerons are called flaperons. And ailerons that do the elevators' job too are called elevons.

Eurofighter EFA 2000

Type: multi-role fighter
Country: UK/Germany/Italy/Spain
Crew: 1
Wingspan: 10.5 metres
Top speed: 2125 kmph (1320 mph)
Max weight: 21,000 kg
Max weapon load: 6500 kg

STEALTH ATTACK

Aircraft can be detected by **radar** long before they can be seen. This makes it very difficult for attack aeroplanes to take their enemy by surprise.

One answer is to fly close to the ground, or behind hills or mountains, where radar doesn't work very well. This is called terrain masking. However, low flying is very dangerous. Aeroplanes risk crashing into hills or being hit by missiles or gunfire from the ground. Another answer is to design an aeroplane so that it can't be found by radar. If the aeroplane is exactly the right shape and covered with the right materials, it disappears from radar screens. An aircraft designed to do this is called a 'stealth' aeroplane. The Lockheed F-117 Nighthawk is one example of a stealth aeroplane. Its body is designed to **disperse** radar waves, so they can't be detected. It is also coated with radar-absorbing materials.

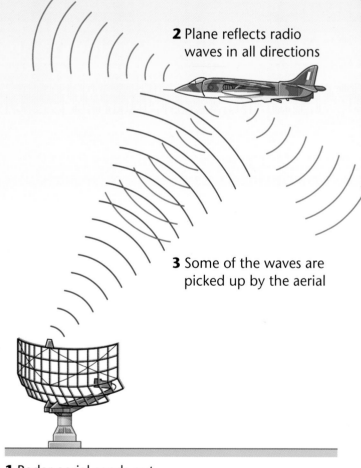

2 Plane reflects radio waves in all directions

3 Some of the waves are picked up by the aerial

1 Radar aerial sends out bursts of radio waves.

RADAR
Radar finds aircraft by sending out radio waves and picking up any waves that are reflected back. It's like throwing a ball – if it bounces back, you know there's something in front of you. The time the ball takes to bounce back tells you how far away it is. Radar works faster than a bouncing ball, because radio waves travel at the speed of light – 300,000 kilometres (186,000 miles) per second!

Lockheed F-117 Nighthawk

Type: stealth attack aircraft

Country: USA

Crew: 1

Wingspan: 13.2 metres

Top speed: 980 kmph (610 mph)

Max weight: 23,815 kg

Max weapon load: 2,270 kg

engines

This Nighthawk has just landed. The parachute is used to slow the plane down.

CARRYING WEAPONS

Attack aeroplanes often hang their weapons underneath their wings and body. The shape of the weapons make the plane easier to detect using radar. The Nighthawk carries its weapons inside its body, so that they don't spoil its carefully designed shape. As it approaches its target, doors in the bottom of the aeroplane's body open and the weapons are released.

HIDING ENGINES

A fighter's engines are very difficult to hide from the enemy. Their heat and the spinning blades can be detected a long way off. The Nighthawk's engines are buried deep inside its wings so that they are more difficult to detect. And the hot **exhausts** from its engines are mixed with cold air to cool them down.

JAGGED EDGE

Every part of the Nighthawk is designed to avoid being detected by radar. Even the edge of the **cockpit** canopy that closes over the pilot is specially designed. It has a jagged edge, because this is more difficult for radar to spot than a straight edge.

LOCKHEED F-22 RAPTOR
TESTING TIMES

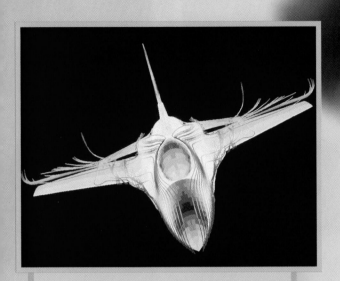

In the 1980s, the US Air Force decided that it needed to begin developing a new fighter to replace its F-15. The US government then asked seven US aeroplane-makers to produce designs.

Two designs, from Lockheed and Northrop, went on to the next stage of the competition. This involved building and testing the two competing aircraft. The Lockheed won and became the F-22 Raptor. The F-22 is a twin-engine jet aeroplane, designed to be more powerful and more **manoeuvrable** than any existing fighter. The shape of its wings and **fuselage** were carefully designed to make the aeroplane hard to find by **radar**. The pilot sits high up, as this gives a clear view all round the aeroplane.

COMPUTER TESTING

Using computers for design and testing saves time and cuts costs. It's called virtual product development. A copy of the aeroplane is created in a computer system. The computer runs tests, called **simulations**, that used to be done by building models and full-size aircraft. The tests show up any parts that don't fit or don't work correctly. These problems are dealt with quickly on the computer screen before any real parts are made.

FLYING TEST-BED

Parts of the F-22 were tested before the aeroplane was built by fitting them to a Boeing 757 airliner. An F-22 **cockpit** was built inside the aeroplane and an F-22 nose was built on the front. An extra wing was added on top. Sensors in the wing were connected to the F-22 instruments and computers that were being tested. Scientists and engineers in the airliner checked how well they worked.

SWIVELLING JETS

The F-22 can do something that most fighters cannot do. The nozzles at the back of its engines swivel up or down when the pilot moves the controls. This is called vectored **thrust** and it makes the aeroplane more manoeuvrable. When both nozzles point upwards, the tail is forced down, the nose rises and the aeroplane climbs. When both nozzles swivel down, the aeroplane dives. When one points up and the other points down, the aeroplane rolls.

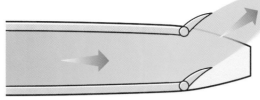

When both nozzles point upwards, the tail of the F-22 is forced down and the aeroplane climbs.

When both nozzles point downwards, the tail is forced up and the aeroplane dives.

The YF-22 was flight-tested at all speeds, heights and angles, even straight up in the air!

THE FIRST F-22

Lockheed's prototype (test model) for the F-22 was called the YF-22. It flew for the first time in 1990. A series of test flights proved that it could do everything the computer simulations predicted it could. The results of the test flights enabled the designers to fine-tune its shape. They made the **tail-fins** smaller and the nose blunter. Then manufacturing could begin.

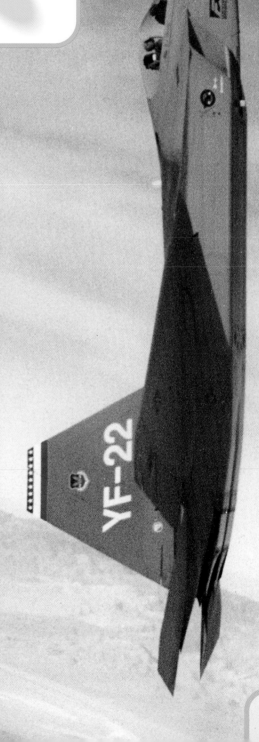

LOCKHEED F-22 RAPTOR
MATERIALS AT THE EDGE

Here the F-22's electronic equipment is being tested by an engineer sitting in the cockpit.

Most fighters are built from aluminium and steel, but the F-22 is different. Its performance depends on using different materials.

Most of the F-22 is made from **titanium** and **composites**. A composite is made from two different materials, which are stronger together than they are separately. Titanium and composites were chosen because they are strong, lightweight and can withstand high temperatures. The aeroplane's main frame is made mainly from titanium. The rest of the aeroplane is built onto this frame. The composite parts are made by laying flexible sheets of composite material on top of each other in a mould. The fabric-like material is then soaked in a liquid plastic, called resin. Finally, the part is cooked in a special oven to harden the resin.

Who makes what?

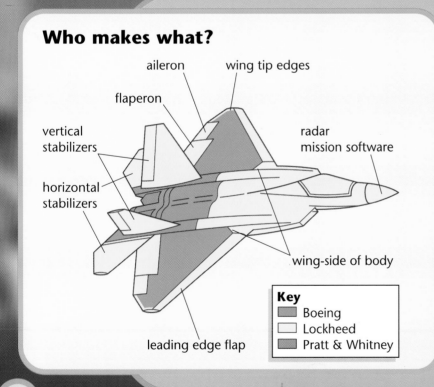

aileron
wing tip edges
flaperon
vertical stabilizers
radar mission software
horizontal stabilizers
wing-side of body
leading edge flap

Key
- ▮ Boeing
- ▯ Lockheed
- ▮ Pratt & Whitney

JOINT EFFORT
Building a fighter is a large and complicated project. It needs so many different skills that several manufacturers work together. The main structure of the F-22 is made by two companies – Lockheed Martin and Boeing. Boeing makes the wings and the tail end of the fuselage. Lockheed Martin makes the rest of the **airframe**. Pratt & Whitney supplies the engines. Hundreds of other companies supply the computers, instruments and other equipment that go inside the aircraft.

FLIGHT COMPUTER

The F-22 is fitted with some of the most advanced avionics (aviation electronics) ever put in an aircraft. It includes a powerful computer to bring all the information from its systems together and present it clearly to the pilot. The F-22's main computer works 100,000 times faster than the computer used in the Apollo Lunar Module that landed the first astronauts on the Moon! It stores 8000 times as much information too.

The F-22's computer might look boring, but it is the world's most advanced high-speed computer system for use in an attack fighter.

COMPUTERIZED COCKPIT

An F-22 pilot sits in front of a bank of computer screens. However, in **combat** the pilot is too busy to look down at them. The most important information is projected onto a glass screen in front of the pilot, called a Head-Up Display (HUD).

F-22 Raptor

Type: advanced tactical fighter
Country: USA
Crew: 1
Wingspan: 13.5 metres
Top speed: more than 2000 kmph (1245 mph)
Max weight: 27,215 kg
Max weapon load: classified

'It [the F-22] is not an airplane you use to defend your airspace. It's an airplane that is used to dominate the other guy's airspace.'
General Ronald R. Fogleman, former Chief of Staff, US Air Force

LOCKHEED F-22 RAPTOR
FAST AND FURIOUS

The F-22 Raptor has an amazing flight performance. It can fly as slow as a small propeller aeroplane or as fast as a **supersonic interceptor**.

Aeroplanes designed to fly at twice the speed of sound are usually very bad at flying slowly. They are the wrong shape. Their wings are designed to work best when they are flying at more than 2000 kph (1245 mph). Amazingly, the F-22 can fly as slowly as a Piper Cub, a small single-engined propeller aeroplane with a top speed of only 140 kph (85 mph). Then it can boost its engines to full power and accelerate to more than **Mach** 2, twice the speed of sound. The F-22 is expected to be in military service by 2005.

COOL DUDE

Fighter pilots work very hard and have to wear a lot of safety clothing while flying. This means they become very hot. So, F-22 pilots have a special cooling layer in their suit. Cool air pumped through this layer carries unwanted heat away from the pilot's body.

INFORMATION OVERLOAD

The pilots of modern fighters are kept busy just making sense of all the information flooding into the cockpit. The F-22's computers sort through it all and show the pilot only the most important information. Several F-22s flying together can also exchange information between their computers automatically, without the pilots having to say a word.

CRAZY ANGLES

The F-22 is designed to be the most agile fighter of all. The pilot can make the aeroplane turn fast enough at all speeds to be able to point and shoot at enemy aircraft. Indeed, the combination of vectored thrust and advanced flight controls enables the F-22 to turn and shoot faster than any aircraft it will ever have to face in combat.

Ernst Mach in around 1890.

MACH NUMBERS

The speed of sound is also called Mach 1. Mach numbers are named after the scientist Ernst Mach, who was interested in what happens to air when something moves through it very quickly. The speed of sound is different in different places. Near the ground, where the air is warm, sound travels at about 1225 kph (760 mph). Higher up, where the air is much colder, the speed of sound falls to about 1000 kph (620 mph).

ENGINE POWER

Fighters are powered by **jet engines**. Small lightweight fighters have one engine. Larger, long-range fighters and heavier fighter-bombers have two engines.

A spinning fan at the front of the engine sucks in air. It passes through more spinning blades, called a compressor. They squash the air before fuel is sprayed into it and burned. This heats the air to more than 1500° Celsius – hot enough to melt iron! Hot air takes up more space than cold air. As the air inside the engine expands, it has to go somewhere. It cannot go forwards because more air is constantly being forced into the engine by the compressor. So, it escapes through the back of the engine as the powerful **exhaust** jet that thrusts the aircraft forwards. On its way, it spins a **turbine** that drives the fan and compressor.

AIR POWER

A jet engine produces its enormous power simply by heating air. This illustration of a Pratt & Whitney F-119-PW-100 engine shows how the process works.

1. Fan sucks cold air in
2. Compressor squashes air
3. Fuel is burned inside the combustion chamber
4. Turbine spins and drives the fan and compressor
5. Air leaves the engine as a hot, fast, exhaust jet

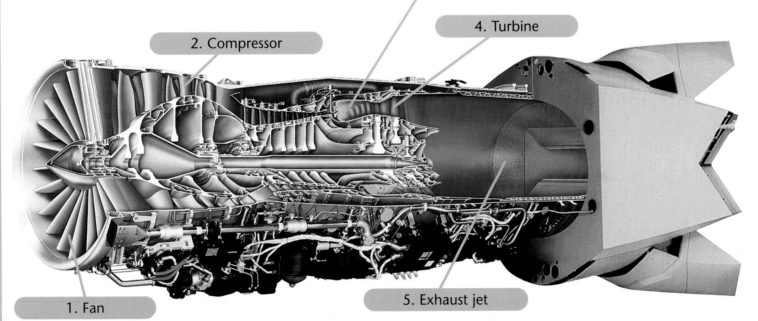

3. Combustion chamber

2. Compressor

4. Turbine

1. Fan

5. Exhaust jet

POWERING THE F-22

The F-22 Raptor is powered by two Pratt & Whitney F119-PW-100 jet engines. They were specially designed for the F-22. They are twice as powerful as any other fighter engine when the aeroplane is flying faster than sound. The engine was designed with advice from the people who will build it and repair it. The result is an engine that is easier to build and quicker to repair than most fighter engines.

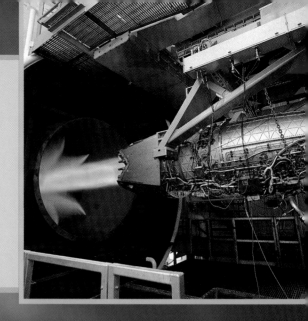

EUROFIGHTER'S ENGINES

The Eurofighter is powered by two EJ200 jet engines. The EJ200 is roughly the same size as the engine that powers the older Tornado fighter-bomber that the Eurofighter will replace. However, the EJ200 has 1000 fewer parts and is 50 per cent more powerful than the Tornado engine. Designers try to build engines with fewer parts, because simpler engines are more reliable.

The F-22 using its afterburners – you can see the flames where the fuel has ignited.

BOOSTING POWER

A fighter engine can be made more powerful by using an afterburner. This sprays fuel into the hot jet coming from the engine. The fuel burns and gives the aeroplane an extra push. Afterburners can help a heavy aeroplane to take off or give an extra burst of speed in **combat**. The F-22 is the only fighter than can fly faster than sound for long periods without using afterburners. This is called supercruise.

NAVY FIGHTERS

The world's largest navies and marine forces have their own fighter aeroplanes. These have to be specially designed or modified for serving on ships.

US Navy fighters like the F-14 Tomcat and F/A-18 Hornet have to withstand the most demanding conditions of any **combat** aircraft. They are based on ships called aircraft carriers that have a runway on the deck. Navy pilots land their aeroplanes by slamming them down hard onto the carrier's deck. A hook in the aeroplane's tail catches a cable strung across the deck and stops the aeroplane. The aeroplane's landing gear has to be made extra-strong to survive these jarring landings, which are more like controlled crashes. Take-offs are hard on navy fighters too. A **catapult** connected to the aeroplane's **nose-wheel** launches it along the deck. Within 3 seconds, it is airborne and doing 250 kph (155 mph).

TOMCAT
A fully laden and fuelled F-14 Tomcat can weigh up to 32 tonnes at take-off. That is as much as 20 small family cars! It works as a **supersonic interceptor** and also as a fighter-bomber carrying heavy weapons. It copes with these different demands by having wings that can move. It is called a 'swing-wing' design, or **variable geometry**. For take-off and landing, its wings stick straight out to the sides. This is the best position for flying slowly.

SWINGING WINGS

Once the Tomcat is in the air, its wings automatically swing backwards to suit its speed. As it flies faster, the wings move back further. At its top speed of about 2500 kph (1555 mph), its wings and tail form a triangular 'delta' shape. This is the best shape for supersonic flight.

Here the Tomcat has its wings swept back in the delta shape.

F-14 Tomcat

Type: navy interceptor/fighter-bomber
Country: USA
Crew: 2
Wingspan: 19.5 metres (max)
Top speed: 2500 kmph (1555 mph)
Max weight: 32,100 kg
Max weapon load: 6,580 kg

FOLDING TIPS

When an F/A-18 Hornet lands on a carrier's deck, its wing-tips begin to fold up. Folding wings make it possible to park aeroplanes closer together and so fit more aeroplanes into the limited space onboard ship. As a Hornet **taxies** to the end of the flight deck for a new mission, its wing-tips unfold again and lock into position, ready for take-off.

JUMP JETS

Nearly all fighters have to move along the ground at high speed before their wings can lift them into the air. Jump jet fighters can fly in a different way.

Jump jets can take off vertically, like a helicopter. They do it by pointing the jet **thrust** from their engine downwards to push the aeroplane upwards. The engine produces **lift** instead of the wings. Then the jets are swivelled backwards and the aeroplane flies off in the normal way. Jump jets can be based almost anywhere, because they don't need a runway. That makes them more difficult for an enemy to find and attack. Vertical take-off uses up so much fuel that jump jets often use a short take-off run to help them to get into the air. This way of using the aeroplane is called **STOVL** (short take-off and vertical landing).

A Harrier takes off from the flight deck of the *USS Saipan* aircraft carrier.

HARRIER II
The first practical jump jet, and the most successful, is the Harrier. The latest model, the Harrier II, is often stationed onboard ships that also carry helicopters. It may take off from a 'ski-jump' at the end of the ship's deck. The ski-jump tips the aeroplane's nose upwards at the end of its take-off run.

A SPECIAL ENGINE

The Harrier needs a special engine for its special flying abilities. A jet engine usually produces one jet of gas that comes straight out of the back of the engine. The Harrier's Pegasus engine produces four jets – two at the front and two at the back. To take off vertically, the pilot turns the four engine nozzles so that they point downwards. The four jets push the aeroplane straight up in the air. To fly forwards, the pilot simply turns the nozzles to point backwards.

HOVER FLYING

An aeroplane is usually steered by moving parts of its wings and tail. This works only when the aeroplane is moving quickly through the air. When a jump jet hovers or takes off vertically, it doesn't move quickly enough to be steered in the normal way. Instead, small jets of air from the engine are blown from the nose, wing-tips and tail to control the aeroplane's position.

Harrier II

Type: STOVL close support aircraft
Country: UK/USA
Crew: 1
Wingspan: 9.3 metres
Top speed: 1065 kmph (660 mph)
Max weight: 14,060 kg
Max weapon load: 6000 kg

Control in a hover

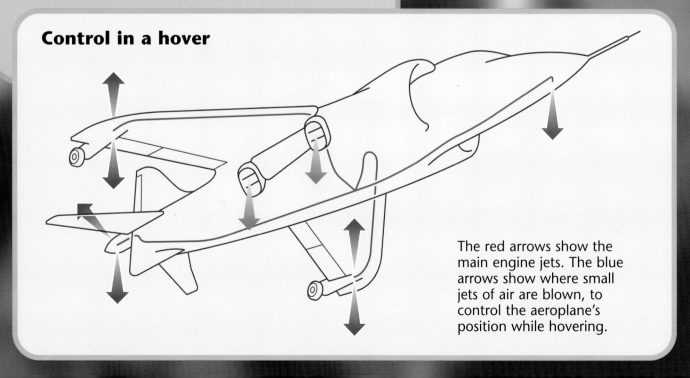

The red arrows show the main engine jets. The blue arrows show where small jets of air are blown, to control the aeroplane's position while hovering.

FLY-BY-WIRE

Modern fighters are flown with the help of computers. Using computers to control aeroplanes in flight has made it possible to design a new type of fighter.

A fighter pilot steers by moving a **stick** like a video game joystick. When the stick moves, computers sense the movement and make the aeroplane do what the pilot wants it to do. It's called fly-by-wire because the controls are connected to the aeroplane's computers by electrical wires. Most aeroplanes fly straight and level if the pilot lets go of the controls. They are said to be stable. The latest fighters are not stable. They would tumble end over end unless their position was corrected every fraction of a second. Their flight computers take care of this vital task automatically. The advantage of making a fighter unstable is that when the pilot wants it to turn, it turns instantly. Making a fighter more **manoeuvrable** like this means that it is more likely to survive an air battle.

FIGHTING FALCON

The F-16 Fighting Falcon was one of the first fly-by-wire fighters. It made its first flight in 1974. It can make amazingly tight turns. The pilot can be forced down into his or her seat so hard in a turn that their body weight feels up to nine times greater than normal. This is called **G-force**. The pilot's arms feel so heavy that it's hard to keep hold of the controls, or even to breathe. However, the F-16 has been so successful that more of them are flown by **Western** air forces than any other fighter.

BACK-SEAT DRIVERS

When a new single-seat fighter like the F-16 is produced, a small number of them are built with two seats in the **cockpit** instead of one. The second seat is used to give experienced fighter pilots their final training on the F-16 before they are allowed to fly one on their own.

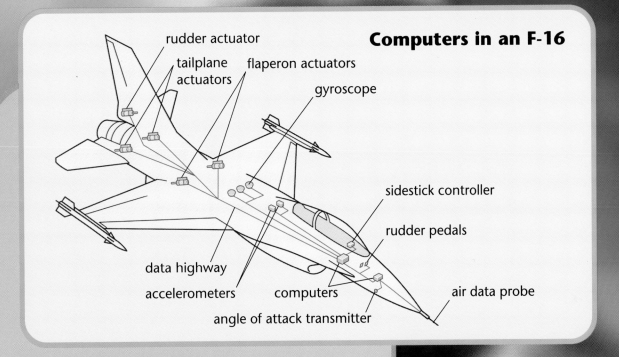

Computers in an F-16

rudder actuator

tailplane actuators

flaperon actuators

gyroscope

sidestick controller

rudder pedals

data highway

accelerometers

computers

angle of attack transmitter

air data probe

COMPUTERS IN CONTROL

The moving parts of a fly-by-wire fighter, such as the **rudder**, are moved by devices called actuators. The actuators are controlled by the aeroplane's computers. The computers need to know how much the aeroplane is turning, diving or climbing, and in which direction, so that they move the actuators by exactly the right amount. This information comes from devices called **accelerometers** and **gyroscopes**. They enable the computers to double-check that the aeroplane is flying as it should.

Lockheed F-16 Fighting Falcon

Type: fighter-bomber

Country: USA

Crew: 1

Wingspan: 10.0 metres

Top speed: 16,875 kmph (1320 mph)

Max weight: 16,875 kg

Max weapon load: 6230 kg

SAFETY FIRST

Fighters cost millions of dollars each, but they can be replaced easily by building more. Fighter crews are much more important and they take years to train. So, they need to be protected as much as possible.

Fighter designers must try to think of every danger the crews might face – and then design aeroplanes to protect them. Some of the safety systems are built into the aeroplane. Others are built into the clothes the crews wear, and even their seats. Most of these safety systems work automatically because the crew may be unable to operate them. In an emergency, if a pilot or weapons officer has to escape from a fighter, there are systems to get them out of the aeroplane quickly and down to the ground safely.

GETTING AIR
The higher you go, the thinner the air gets. Fighters often fly thousands of metres above the ground. At that height, the air is too thin to breathe. Fighter pilots wear a mask that supplies them with **oxygen**. The mask also contains a **microphone** connected to the fighter's radio.

DRESSING FOR WORK

Fighter crews wear a special suit called a partial pressure suit, or G-suit. When a fighter turns sharply, the **G-force** pushes the blood down out of the pilot's head. If the brain doesn't receive enough blood, it is starved of oxygen and the result is a black-out. The G-suit prevents this by squeezing the legs, which stops blood draining into them. F-15 and F-16 pilots also wear a pressurized breathing system. In tight turns, the pilot breathes high-pressure air. At the same time, a vest is inflated to balance the pressure on the outside of the chest.

STAYING AFLOAT

All fighter pilots wear a life preserver. If a pilot has to parachute into the sea, the life preserver automatically inflates and keeps the pilot afloat. A pilot may land unconscious in water, so it's important that the life preserver turns him onto his back to keep his face out of the water.

ROCKET SEATS

If a fighter is about to crash, the crew has no choice but to get out of the aeroplane. Each crew-member sits in a special seat called an ejector seat. To eject, he or she pulls a handle. A rocket in the seat fires, blasting it clear of the aeroplane. The crew-member is out of the aeroplane within half a second and floats to the ground by parachute.

FAST AND FURIOUS

The designers who create fighters and attack aeroplanes for air forces and navies have produced some amazing machines.

Every time a new fighter or attack aeroplane is built, other air forces and navies around the world study it. If they think their own aeroplanes or ground defences can't defeat it, they may develop a new aeroplane of their own. It's a long process. For example, from the time the USA decided to build the F-22 until it enters service, the whole design and testing process will have taken 25 years. The cost, in both money and effort, is enormous. But whoever designs the planes, they have to come up with their own unique solutions to the design problem.

SU-27 FLANKER

The Russian Sukhoi Su-27 is one of the world's best fighters. When it first appeared in air displays, its abilities astonished everyone. A manoeuvre called the 'cobra' is very popular. The fighter flies normally, then the nose suddenly tips up until the aeroplane is standing on its tail, still flying forwards. Then the nose falls forward again and the aeroplane flies on. It's called the cobra because it looks like a cobra snake rearing up.

TANK-BUSTER

Not all attack fighters have to be super fast. The top speed of the American A-10 Thunderbolt II is only 700 kph (435 mph), but speed is not important. The A-10 is designed to fly close to the ground and attack tanks and other armoured vehicles. Because it flies so low and slow, it is designed to survive a lot of damage. It can fly home even if one engine is shot away altogether! The pilot sits in an armoured 'bathtub' for protection against attack from below.

Smoke pours from an A-10 Thunderbolt as the pilot fires the big seven-barrelled tank-busting gun in the plane's nose.

A-10 Thunderbolt II

Type: anti-armour close support attack aeroplane
Country: USA
Crew: 1
Wingspan: 17.5 metres
Top speed: 700 kmph (435 mph)
Max weight: 22,680 kg
Max weapon load: 7250 kg

FUTURE FIGHTER

The next American attack aircraft is already being designed. At first, it was called the Joint Strike Fighter. When Lockheed Martin was chosen to build it, it became known as the F-35. While the F-22 concentrates on **combat** with other aircraft, the F-35 will attack ground targets. There will be three versions of the aircraft. The Air Force will fly the standard version. The Navy version will have bigger wings and a stronger structure for landing on a carrier deck. The **Marine Corps** version will be a **STOVL** (short take-off and vertical landing) aircraft.

DATA FILES

The main fighters in service with armed forces all over the world are listed below.

Attack fighter aeroplane	Country of origin	Wingspan (metres)	Top speed (kmph / mph)	Max take-off weight (kgs)	Weapons load (kgs)
A-10 Thunderbolt II anti-armour close support attack aeroplane	USA	17.5	700 / 435	22,680	7250
Eurofighter EFA2000 multi-role fighter	Europe	10.5	2125 / 1320	21,000	6500
F-14 Tomcat navy interceptor/fighter-bomber	USA	19.5	2500 / 1555	32,100	6580
F-15E Strike Eagle strike fighter-bomber	USA	13.1	2655 / 1650	36,740	11,110
F-16 Fighting Falcon fighter-bomber	USA	10.0	2125 / 1320	16,875	6230
F/A-18 Hornet fighter-bomber	USA	12.3	1915 / 1190	23,540	7030
F-22 Raptor advanced tactical fighter	USA	13.5	2000+ / 1245+	27,215	classified
F-117 Nighthawk stealth attack aircraft	USA	13.2	980 / 610	23,815	2270
Gripen JAS 39 multi-role fighter	Sweden	8.0	2125 / 1320	12,475	6500
Harrier II STOVL close-support aircraft	UK/USA	9.3	1065 / 660	14,060	6000
MiG-25 Foxbat interceptor	Russia	14.1	3395 / 2110	41,000	4000
Rafale multi-role fighter	France	10.9	2125 / 1320	24,500	6000
Sukhoi Su-27 Flanker multi-role fighter	Russia	14.7	2500 / 1555	30,000	8000
Tornado IDS interdictor strike aircraft	Europe	13.9	1480 / 920	27,950	9000

Attack fighters have advanced a great deal since the days of this British Sopwith Camel fighter used during the First World War (1914–1918).

FURTHER READING AND RESEARCH

BOOKS

Collins Gem: Combat Aircraft, Collins, 2001
Fighter Aircraft, by Francis Crosby, Lorenz Books, 2002
Fighter Planes, by Bill Gunston, Tick Tock Publishing, 1999
Modern Air Combat, by Bill Gunston and Mike Spick, Salamander Books, 1983
The History of Aviation, by Dennis Baldry, Chancellor Press, 1999
The World's Great Stealth and Reconnaissance Aircraft, W H Smith Exclusive Books, 1991

MAGAZINE ARTICLES

'The Greatest!', *Focus*, May 1996, an article about the Eurofighter

WEBSITES

You can find out more about the world's fighter aeroplanes by looking at the
following websites. Some of them are provided by the companies that manufacture
fighters and their engines. Others are provided by museums that specialize in aviation.

http://www.lmaeronautics.com
Website of Lockheed Martin Aerospace, manufacturer of the F-117 Nighthawk and
F-22 Raptor combat planes.

http://www.boeing.com
Website of Boeing Aerospace, manufacturer of parts of the F-22 Raptor.

http://www.pratt-whitney.com
Website of fighter engine manufacturer Pratt & Whitney.

http://www.eurofighter.com/home.asp
Website devoted to the Eurofighter.

http://www.nasm.edu
Website of the US National Air and Space Museum.

http://www.utc.com/discover/hiw-eng.htm
A guide to how a jet engine works.

By the 1940s, fighters such as this American P-51 Mustang
could fly at speeds of up to 600 kph (373 mph).

GLOSSARY

accelerometer a device that measures acceleration

ailerons moving parts of a fighter's wings. When one aileron tilts up and the other tilts down, the aeroplane rolls.

airframe the body of an aircraft without its engines

air-superiority fighter a fighter designed to seek out enemy planes and clear them from the sky. This means that troops can move about freely on the ground without suffering air attacks.

catapult equipment fitted to an aircraft carrier to launch combat aeroplanes along the deck

cockpit part of an aircraft where the pilot sits. Some fighters have a second cockpit where a weapons officer sits.

combat fighting

composite material used to build parts of fighters. A composite is made from two different materials that become stronger when combined. One type of composite is made from carbon fibre soaked in sticky liquid resin, which then hardens.

control surfaces the parts of an aeroplane's wings and tail that are moved by the pilot to steer the aeroplane

disperse to scatter something over a wide area

dogfight close combat between fighters chasing each other through the sky

elevators moving parts of a fighter's tail. Elevators change an aeroplane's pitch – when the elevators tilt up or down, the aeroplane climbs or dives.

exhaust the hot gases that rush out of an engine

fuselage body of an aeroplane. A fighter's fuselage contains the engine, or engines, and the cockpit.

G-force a force equal to one or more times the force of gravity

gyroscope a device made from a spinning disc. When an aeroplane turns or tilts, gyroscopes inside it stay in the same position. This enables computers to keep track of an aeroplane's movements.

interceptor type of fighter designed to stop the approach of enemy fighters or bombers

jet engine type of engine that produces a high-speed jet of gas to thrust an aircraft forwards

lift a force, acting upwards, that is produced by an aeroplane's wings or a helicopter's rotor blades as they cut through the air

Mach number aircraft's speed divided by the speed of sound. Mach 1 is the speed of sound. Mach 2 is twice the speed of sound.

manoeuvrable/manoeuvrability ability to turn this way and that with ease

Marine Corps a branch of the US armed forces composed of sea-going troops

microphone the part of a fighter's radio system that lets the pilot talk to people. It changes the pilot's voice into an electric current. A microphone is built into the pilot's helmet.

nose-wheel a plane's landing wheel underneath its nose

oxygen one of the gases that make up air

radar Radio Detection and Ranging, a method for finding distant objects by sending out radio waves and picking up any reflections that bounce back

rudder the part of a fighter's tail-fin that swivels to the left and right to turn the aeroplane's nose left or right. Turning to the left and right is also called yaw.

simulation a copy of a problem or situation created inside a computer. A whole aircraft can be created, or modelled, in a computer. It can then be tested to see how the real aeroplane will fly in different conditions and at different speeds.

stick short for 'control stick' or 'joystick', the main flying control in a small aircraft's cockpit. Moving the stick in any direction makes the plane tilt in that way.

STOVL Short Take-Off and Vertical Landing. A STOVL plane takes off after a very short take-off run and it can land vertically, like a helicopter.

supersonic faster than the speed of sound

tail-fin the part of an aircraft that stands up at the rear end. It keeps the plane's tail steady and stops it from swinging about from side to side.

tail-planes small wing-like parts on either side of an aeroplane's tail

taxiing when an aircraft moves along the ground under its own power

thrust the force produced by an engine to propel an aircraft

titanium a strong lightweight metal that withstands very high temperatures and doesn't rust. Titanium is often used to make parts of the fastest aeroplanes.

turbine part of a jet engine that is spun by the jet of gas rushing out of the engine. The spinning turbine drives the engine's fan and compressor.

variable geometry 'swing-wing'. A variable geometry, or swing-wing, plane can make its wings stick straight out to the side for flying slowly and then swing them back to form a slender dart-like shape for flying fast.

Western concerning north American and western European countries